THE SILENCE OF MY ROOM

THE SILENCE OF MY ROOM

poems by GUY R. BEINING

Published by Chintamani Books
P.O. Box 131, Planetarium Station
New York, NY 10024
ISBN 978-0-9960236-4-1

Copyright © Guy R. Beining, 2018

Printed in the United States of America
in accordance with the Sustainable Forestry Initiative.

Table of Contents

poem i	9
poem ii	10
poem iii	11
poem iv	12
poem v	13
poem vi	14
poem vii	15
poem viii	16
poem ix	17
poem x	18
poem xi	19
poem xii	20
poem xiii	21
poem xiv	22
poem xv	23
poem xvi	24
poem xvii	25
poem xviii	26
poem xix	27
poem xx	28
poem xxi	29
poem xxii	30
poem xxiii	31
poem xxiv	32
poem xxv	33
poem xxvi	34
poem xxvii	35
poem xxvii	36
poem xxix	37
poem xxx	38

poem xxxi	39
poem xxxii	40
poem xxxiii	41
poem xxxiv	42
poem xxxv	43
poem xxxvi	44
poem xxxvii	45
poem xxxviii	46
poem xxxix	47
poem xl	48
poem xli	49
poem xlii	50
poem xliii	51
poem xliv	52
poem xlv	53
poem xlvi	54
poem xlvii	55
poem xlviii	56
poem xlix	57
poem l	58
poem li	59
poem lii	60
poem liii	61
poem liv	62
poem lv	63
poem lvi	64
poem lvii	65
poem lviii	66
poem lix	67
poem lx	68
poem lxi	69
ACKNOLWEDGEMENTS	71
BOOKS BY THE AUTHOR	75

*To Anna my wife
who has woven the skies of our dwellings
with the perfect rain cloud tapestry.*

i.

are you open
to the rattling world
one step out
of its frozen past?
i am now circling with
saturn feet, copying
something unwell in
the hexagon of
a hive where humans
nest incomplete in
jargon & jarring
forces, with dust
from earlier metals
ringing their minds shut.

ii.

chapter 1 begins:
it was a
choice of
three states—
the chair,
the gas & the rope,
or just to be off
with his head.
he had used
a razor—
no, it was a gun,
but really a scarf
that she had
wound too tightly.

iii.

a sea of stars
(in a tide)
were pushed to
one side of
the blackboard sky
in seminal scatterings
without a view
in a giant
end of every-
thing, within the
sleeve of this
formal stage.
to what preamble
perambulating does the night
window touch a skull?

iv.

making lines
before coffee
had a pot,
opening daybreak
with the blue
key of midnight,
moving between
silver strokes
of seconds &
measuring the length of
descent
in the long hall-
way of short endings—
there was a
matter of muttering,
of calling the
crowd within one.

v.

caption a night
of fighting
with loose
ends—a trampled
morning diagrammed
on the blackboard.
the statement is set within
harsh brackets,
now jarred
beyond the point
of speaking, while
wheels
travel far off.

vi.

how do we
wear
the head?
it is not elegant
& falls into
shadow quickly,
so back up
my sinking noggin,
my lost identity.
bring me
marbles which
i'll play out
in this back-
ground game.

vii.

let's scribble
on the plates
of the rich—
something like this:
eat the hand
that pulls the plug.
or let's break
down houses
made out of glass
& look for
the princess of
processed images &
say farewell to
the long-legged
goose that trims
the pants off
a carefree few.

viii.

a stream of
make-believe actions
operate on
low voltage—
the script,
a summary of doubts.
trying to take
apart the weed
filled path, i see
eyes flutter.
better to hide
in shadows,
to limp past bureaus
full of old images.
the poet as actor,
as imposter, as
visual glue-maker,
becomes a spider
in a deep
dark cellar.

ix.

something was left
out of the chapter
in the blotter of time.
something spilled
over in trickling
conversation and was
left in the hollow
speak-easy quality
of a bar.
all the black
stools were
shiny & empty,
as a slow
mop spread over
the floor.

x.

the pushcart
was pulled
by a thief,
a spectacled
academic with
leaden feet.
the wagon
was battered
& the round
clay head
of the leading
thinker stumbled
over a rock.
as he fell
forward, his head
split open revealing
nothing but
straw matter.

xi.

the merry boat-
swain chuckled
in the sunlight
as the waters
carried him past
gulf & mobile
signs into
the flatlands
of america.
here is the plains state
where all the moveable
forests have long
since gone
& all those little
known tracks have
been molded into pots.

xii.

he would whistle
in the parsonage.
be tidy now
he'd say, walking
out of light, walking
from rows of houses
& walking into the
rain of writing with
pockets to gather
the taste of the seasons.

dust, twigs, earth,
leaves & water fall
thru vacuous hands.

xiii.

there is a
wheelbarrel lane
for outcast poets
who bargain with
nothing but what is
twice a question,
later stated.
it is time
to go to the parlor.
pardon the block-
age of the hour,
but are we
moving at all?

xiv.

going to the end
of a long line
(the end of one's
unknown property),
sifting thru remnants
of things that once
had meaning,
trying to file down
the thoughts of
those days—

it's not easy
to throw away
half-truths if
one can't find
building blocks
or signs of
where it all began.

xv.

the colors on a map
fill geographics:
brown-edged mountains,
a split bolt
or two &
a smudged imprint
of humanity
in the pink.

we know we have
lost the trail,
the trek thru
tracks crushed.
no moan
will break the spell.

xvi.

pick the room;
pick the bed.
it's time to turn
over the last card
& make plain
what blankness is:
a nothing face
avoids voices lost,
tries to escape
the tracks of
a bad movie
& now sits on
the balcony of
a bright, white
hotel, hoping
to find a way
into its sullenness.

xvii.

one hears
overstatements on light
& beginnings.
all daily
habits are sad &
in the front lines of
everywhere, there is
gazing.

watching an obscure car
jitter in a glass garage,
the mechanic sits idly,
tho once he fenced engines.
several rooms away,
a knob turns
& the wheels
begin to spin.

xviii.

there is no-
thing here but
strangeness &
the finishing of wings.
the grin of a camel
slowly disappears.

i will wear
my very rosy hat
& calf skin knickers
& be a dodger,
holding onto fenders,
barking to the trainer
in the glow of kings.

xix.

this is more
of an inside
question with
no color displayed.
up the narrow path
they go, straight
into flying tickets
from the war machine,
so i ask:

why does the head
of a nation
only nod, almost cower,
waiting for the tail
to whack the neck?

xx.

in the reeds
there was a word.
dirt, salt & roots
changed &
the rain circled
to become a pond.
nature's coat was
slowly torn apart,
as the stong scent
of flowers disappeared.

take all
good things back
& leave the rest.

xxi.

i am the leaf
that will not fall,
tho autumn
rushes about me
& my mind
clings to the cool
stones below.
there is no
boundary for the
poet in any
season, so row
me out into
the dark mirrored
look of the lake
& call for plans
less tragic.

xxii.

somewhere down
the road—
a porch light.
time has too
quickly passed,
leaving me in
yesterday's ditch.
i am gnawing at
the stem of creation,
sowing along the lines
of another season.
piano notes
still the air
& i remember how
i used to bend
back so far
as to see the world.

xxiii.

you have a speech,
a subject of being
& you're on
the prattle line,
the point where
boiling is temperate;
so don't stumble
& ignore your skull
bobbling in a fish tank,
where the light is so sweet,
yellow-green & silent.

xxiv.

the world ends
again as a goat
chews away at
your last shirt.
in the theatre
(movie house) of
the 20th century,
no one can
reach the light.
it is expected
to appear on
a giant computer
screen, making a
halloween,
fixing the gravel
path in the zen quantum
triangular approach.

xxv.

someone introduced me
to the silence
of my room
by leaving sand-
bags all around
my desk. one sits
on top of my
writing machine
that no longer
hums. the stand-

in ghosts
of winter go over
the spasms of the season
& finally etch
a dead sheep with a
mature countenance.

xxvi.

in my coney island
days i coughed
outside of liquor stores.
my fiery head
looked up at
solarcaine billboards.
nothing much to sort out then,
but now the mind is
walking past eddies,
past fascination's parlor.
across surf avenue, there
are poster games,
fingers fast
on the draw.

xxvii.

the day appears
to have been
sandpapered out
of existence.
the mind brushes
maps made by birds &
sectioned-out pieces
of the moon
are snapped together,
creating model cities
where no one walks.
the next step
would be star trips,
predatory years of
black, blank space,
a depth of no depth.

xxviii.

barely off center
miniature turtles
circle the spot,
holding
onto each glass wave.
minnows, tight as
water, find the sunspot &
proof-read
the universal pulse.

we are all tampered with,
as we watch
the tinny night turn
a silver train
over the continental shelf
without a sigh.

xxix.

at the boxed
black theatre,
entertainers
have been known
to drown in
curtains going up.
liquor slips, love
slips & the pointed
ray that is life
slips.

she crept into
his seat, tho no-
thing magical
happened.

xxx.

come to the floor show:
small questions talk
with lawless walks &
wide movements
in confounded light.
they are bright
in being lucid,
making small circles,
weighing carved instruments,
pulling at shuttered bones,
moving toward the
scalped works of a nation.

xxxi.

fingering what I
know of you,
I yank
the feet
of the poem
off of the tar mat
& the crystal
head sags at
its center, letting
exposure float.

xxxii.

the matchbox stage
shines in your eyes
& empties the night,
as dust lifts.
small games are
unpacked in the meadow,
among sounds of insects
squeezing out comfort.
stars prick
all those that climb
ashen hills
with pockets full
of jewels.

xxxiii.

being in the eve,
being in the green
smoke, being of
rock & tree—

a figure not
meant to be
more than a blind
spot in the
universal pull,
i am always in that
passage between tide
& pulse, a sand
bar of another era,
something unbrushed,
unknown.

xxxiv.

the clouds are
ready to
move forward
set by sea & sin.
there is more
on the line than
we could
find in the end.

we say the mud
is moving,
but no—
the manatee
is moving along the creek.

XXXV.

having crossed &
watched brown
marshes dim out
the landscape,
dragonflies skirt
the pier.

figures near the lake
dodge summer's buzzings
& the shadow of
a mammal gets closer.

shut the might door;
shut the mighty head.

xxxvi.

the dialogue falls
like cement &
puddles of light
arm the territory.
parts of a riddle
swirl in a pot.

after coffee, plausible
thoughts develop,
tho words are muffled by
an opus of birds.
nothing falls out
of the darkness
except a screech.

xxxvii.

a frame is
slipped over the view
in the peacock room.
everything is placed,
as if on a shelf.
nuanced sentences burble
up under a table lamp.
another centerpiece
will be needed.
a toe moves forward
changing the demeanor
of the hostess.

xxxviii.

from the pier,
night fishes the sky.
see a rafter on
the bridge
of the moon,
tho no key fits.
from the gazebo,
morning begins to
press wet jewels.
the spoken word
has broken up &
like an animal,
sounds are hurled out
past countless fields.

xxxix.

point one
is not to be
found.
a tray
slipped.
trash & all
the blind
points, as in
two or any
slow number,
are taking
us over.

xl.

back to back:
he points
to muddy tracks
all about
an unlevel
development.
signs everywhere
throw him back.

so much
fun—
not knowing
where to put
one's foot.

xli.

so mend the foot
& treatise
all abaft,
ie. to be in the rear
of our awareness.
there to find
sniveling a willowy
lady without wears
(impish)
& a dish to break
bread with,
or cut thru the matter
of nakedness
in the lily pond.

xlii.

a new morning—
lyrics tapping at
the windowpane
that is far off.
o, a problem with
musicality.
out of theatrical air
rise fiddlers fit,
pouring several quarts
of crushing disorder.

xliii.

all abash,
but up
to snuff.
being in one's
own world
is all we can ask,
except for food,
ties or plenty
of pencils &
a desk that does not shine

& to catch oneself
as one is.

xliv.

the exceptional
rant will
disappear,
yet for it to abate
the wolf in the head
must turn to particles,
tho that is
begging the question.

a word ladder
approaches at a
frightful angle,
putting to bed
any recovery.

xlv.

sun is
forgotten
fire in the thick
walls of winter.
a cracked abode,
now a stage,
bare.
bone
drums
sound
again & again
& all
the picture windows
blow apart.

xlvi.

the final
set of lines
fell off
the table.
where do we
go from here?

perhaps abort,
go into hiding,
or dig into
middle grounds,
pouring out
sounds &
symbols of sounds,
yet not dropping
the seeds of verse.

xlvii.

in praise
of dirt:
fair or unfair
we move,
muddling the
muck about us.
can one
put a pencil
to it,
or a solid
line 'round it?
playing with
the fingers
of what
is above, we
splinter pieces
of perfect music.

xlviii.

we are growing into
the season
of make
believe life.
corporeal questions
nudge concerns
about the wintry
flight of geese.
now, the acrid
days of stone
& dumb drumming
of leaves
put one into
a delicious dearth
that turns
the apple cart.

xlix.

ecliptical mode is
semi-arid, semi-
circular, so put
to rest
the broker's tongue
slushing in verbal
flimflam. we are
unable to adapt.

o, our hours,
once safe as a nun's
belief,
now tumble like
so many bricks.

l.

i want
to grieve
at your doorstep
& turn all the
lightning bugs into
fractions of a god,
or make a splash.
the last
curtain of life falls.
there is nothing
to be added or put
on the shelf.

li.

hearing the crush
of fire & disorder,
i wake up
to be adept
at tracing
& retracing the
holes that develop
in stone. i note
the disappearance
of mirrored glass,
reflecting & refracting
a decade
gone deeper
then sad.

lii.

small bits of light
play
smoothly upon him.
he sees a gun &
the arrow
of a head
but will not
admit to
bad dreams;
tho he hears
footfalls over
footprints as
powder of
the moon settles.

liii.

he mutters
to the soft
remnants of
his life, to
the parts he
has long since
pulled to shreds.
he will make
a small seat
out of sand,
sit all afire &
wait for the
right story to
cover him up.

liv.

he ignored
the effrontery
of history:
what do you
want to say
before you die?
well, it was
a swell tour,
tho never very
fashionable &
full of unwanted
goods.

being
a tourist puts
one far from any
real connection.

lv.

aisle to aisle,
the rumbling feet
move with no
text to turn
the head.

butting bees align
for honey &
stirred by degrees
see that life
is fed to no one
without work
of a queen.

lvi.

the moon rises
like a disabling shot
over the moor.
dark water &
the years like
worn ropes
hang about one.
each knuckle of
a word raps
the narrowing front
door & in the back
room of verse,
songs spring apart.

lvii.

a girl watches
her penmanship
fall apart, while
one mystery falls
on top of another:

i should pull
the skirt off
your nose
the sailor said to her,
or was it
the marionette that
he spoke to?
& then there was the
fellow with an alias.

distance becomes a
matter of insight.

lviii.

a bird splinters and
lands like a bonfire.
where was the abyss
of its bath?

going down a silvery
lane, with the taste
of mint clinging to his
sunday wears, is the parson.
he adjusts his glasses as
he passes the spot of
broken wings & promises.

lvix.

i can not crack
the code of insiders,
those dastardly
worms that rotate
all amuck,
all amiss,
crawling slowly into
a mower's light,
tapping the last
scent of autumn,
following a line
of white mushrooms.

lx.

there is a long
spill
along the coast
spitting fire to the shoreline,
so drive past empty chairs
& a line full
of heads diving under.

music
becomes a palace
to the sun, reaching
for the circumference of light.
it's time to wake up my pretty.

lxi.

my light blue tie
shines like the sea.
i go tripping—
i go
tripping not
remembering.
i see you largely
there in the
jar of your light.

memory once had
me there & i flew
like a perfect bee.

ACKNOWLEDGEMENTS

The author is grateful to the editors of the following journals where several of these poems first appeared.

Chiron Review
ii

Verse Wisconsin
v
lv

Minotaur
ix
xv-xvi

Spring
xvii

Lalitamba
xxxiii

Big Hammer
lii

BOOKS BY THE AUTHOR

The Raw-Robed Few (Long Beach: Applezaba Press, 1982)

100 Haiku Selected from a Decade (Houston: O!!Zone Press, 1993)

Too Far To Hear (Buffalo: Leave Books, 1994)

Carved Erosion (Seattle: Elbow Press, 1995)

The Compact Duchamp (Cincinnati: Chapultepec Press, 2003)

Out of the Wood into the Sun (Stockholm: Kamini Press, 2011)

I Guess My Loss Is Almot Grey (New York: Rain Mountain Press, 2016)

www.ingramcontent.com/pod-product-compliance
Lightning Source LLC
Chambersburg PA
CBHW051702040426
42446CB00009B/1256